THINK AGAIN
BEFORE YOU SAY
"I DO"

LEON BOGLE

WESTBOW
PRESS®
A DIVISION OF THOMAS NELSON
& ZONDERVAN

This book is a work of non-fiction. Unless otherwise noted, the author and the publisher make no explicit guarantees as to the accuracy of the information contained in this book and in some cases, names of people and places have been altered to protect their privacy.

WestBow Press books may be ordered through booksellers or by contacting:

WestBow Press
A Division of Thomas Nelson & Zondervan
1663 Liberty Drive
Bloomington, IN 47403
www.westbowpress.com
844-714-3454

Because of the dynamic nature of the Internet, any web addresses or links contained in this book may have changed since publication and may no longer be valid. The views expressed in this work are solely those of the author and do not necessarily reflect the views of the publisher, and the publisher hereby disclaims any responsibility for them.

Any people depicted in stock imagery provided by Getty Images are models, and such images are being used for illustrative purposes only.
Certain stock imagery © Getty Images.

All Scripture quotations are taken from the King James Version.

ISBN: 978-1-6642-5235-6 (sc)
ISBN: 978-1-6642-5234-9 (hc)
ISBN: 978-1-6642-5236-3 (e)

Library of Congress Control Number: 2021924853

Print information available on the last page.

WestBow Press rev. date: 12/15/2021

This could be the most life changing book you'll ever read. Pastor Leon Bogle's book, "Think Again Before You Say I Do", sets out for its readers comprehensive guidelines for a successful marriage. Though not exhaustive, this book offers intangible information for those seeking to be engaged in marriage for a lifetime. "Think Again Before You Say I Do" answers questions which will preserve your marriage and strengthen your love relationship. Pastor Leon has written from a biblical and personal view and experience. His candid exposition will guide his readers to be both honest and informed. (The Book) "Think Again Before You Say I Do" will also keep you from trying to correct avoidable mistakes often made by uninformed couples. Well done Pastor Bogle.

Errol Campbell, Pastor of Victory Family Fellowship International Ministries and CCAL Member of Canada.

Acknowledgments

Thanks to my beautiful wife, Zelpher, to whom I have been married for twenty-two years and who has given me three wonderful children: my son Ephraim, and my daughters Alexandrina and Loudonya.

Thanks also to my son Damian and daughter Jevonia. Thank you, Zelpher, for all the time you have surrendered—time we otherwise would have spent together socially. Thanks for your support and all the help you gave to help me become who I am today. With God's help and your support, I have been able to find success in ministry.

To God I give all my honor and glory for His favor and grace.

I pray that every reader will be blessed and inspired by this book.

INTRODUCTION

As the ninth child of my father, Loren, and the fourth of my mother, Mervis, I was born on the island of Jamaica, in the parish of Saint Thomas, in the community of Aeolus Valley.

Growing up was, as is the case with many children of the world, very challenging. There were the normal challenges of school and community, and there were the challenges I had to face within our home.

The reason for this book, *Think Again before You Say "I do"*, I would say, has its foundation in the experiences I had while growing up with my mom and dad. These were two lovely people with very flawed character traits. It is evident to me now that my parents had no idea how negatively certain actions of theirs were impacting us, their children. My dad was well beloved in the community; he was a police officer with a very friendly disposition. He was never too busy to take time out for counseling anyone who would seek his advice. You might call him the community social worker. My mom, on the other, hand was more focused on what mattered for her and those she chose to care for. However, it is true that all that glitters is not gold. You see, while on the outside in the community my dad was celebrated, there were parts of his character that were always in question. How could the most cordial, friendly community personality be the same person who was the community drunk? How could he be one of the men who were unfaithful to their wives? And how could this man who was friendly to everyone not find peace with his wife?

In our home, there were always disagreements; a friendly man and an unhappy wife who was naturally unfriendly to everyone who was not part of her own family were not a comfortable combination. Yes, my dad was kind, friendly, and a peace officer, but he was also a wasteful spender. His free spending and our mother's social and fiscal conservativeness were always at odds, not to mention his promiscuous lifestyle.

There were those of the community who questioned his fidelity to our mother. My siblings and I several times met other children in the community who bore so strong a family resemblance to us that we, as children of our father, would question whether or not these were other siblings of ours.

The frequent disagreements and verbal fights between our parents were so impacting that I have a vivid recollection of an older brother of mine once asking my dad why he married our mom. Not only did our dad have these unsavory behaviors, but our mom was also a controlling and difficult character. All these things, plus the observations I made after seeing the lifestyle patterns of other couples, led me to question whether there was anything called a happy marriage.

As the product of an unfaithful father, I became an unfaithful man. It seemed natural to me to practice what I had seen other men do. When I grew up, I dated several women at the same time, and having had sexual encounters with each of them seemed natural and okay. This was a lifestyle legacy of home and community. My encounter with Jesus Christ changed it all. Now I have developed a godly perspective about intimacy and marriage. It is therefore my sincere hope and desire that those who read this book will conclude that it is truly wise to think again before they say, "I do."

CHAPTER 1

In Pursuit of Marriage

It is an irrefutable fact that choices have consequences. Marriage is an institution that produces great challenges, and once we are in it, these challenges are inescapable. The impact of these challenges, negative or positive, can oftentimes be determined by the decisions made before marriage happens. *Think Again before You Say "I Do"* will discuss many of these issues that need to be addressed before entering into marriage.

In this book I will share some of my personal experiences—ones that can help you to avoid some of the pitfalls that so many have stumbled over only because they did not make the right decisions or have the necessary discussions before entering into marriage. It is important to understand that no amount of discussions held on any subject will ease the pain that can come with marriage if the parties are not willing to live up to the agreements made. Discussions are not meant to be had just so two people can get married. Meaningful discussions are designed to be a road map for the future. When positive discussions are held and the parties honor the agreements arrived at through those discussions, then the parties involved are more likely to experience the true joys of marriage.

We've all heard that experience teaches wisdom, so I'll share some of my experiences with you.

After observing many unpleasant and difficult interactions between married couples before I got married, I had my own thoughts of what a marriage should be like. I even asked questions of and gave advice to several couples while believing that I could do better in marriage than they were doing. What I did not consider was that choices made without proper counsel and preplanning are more likely to result in disastrous experiences. Marriage is more than just one's love for the physical features of another.

I was born in a family where my dad and my mom were constantly at war with each other, and I was sure that I would do better than that. I came to Canada from Jamaica, and after living in circumstances where the lifestyles of husbands and wives were carbon copies of my childhood experiences, I found myself a beautiful young lady to whom I got married after a short period of time.

We had no significant discussions about what life in marriage should look like. We just got married because we were in love. The union produced one child. It was not long after our marriage before we were at each other, constantly bickering, because there was no foundation set for understanding our roles in marriage. We began seeing all the flaws that we either previously chose to ignore or were oblivious to during our times of dating and courtship.

We were so different in our approaches to so many things that were important—things that we needed to agree on if our marriage was to survive. We did not agree on parenting, financial management, or even how individuals are to coexist as a family, let alone with a child. After separating from each other for a while and living in separate cities, we subsequently got divorced.

Although I contemplated just living alone, finding someone to love, and not getting married, I soon fell into the same trap once again. "Old habits die hard," they say. One day while walking in the park in Edmonton, Alberta, I saw a beautiful young lady named Zelpher, whose parents I knew from living in Jamaica. I was immediately captivated by her smile, light complexion, and beautiful bold eyes. After some discussions with this young lady and my stating my special admiration of her, she made it clear that she was not interested in me and, as a matter of fact, did not like me even as much as her smallest fingernail. However, her approach to choosing a mate was no different from mine. She wanted a man who was tall, handsome, and could sing. These are not necessarily the prerequisites for a wholesome marriage. Neither her stated requirements nor the fact that she said she didn't care for me stopped me from pursuing a relationship with her. Back in those days, not many people had cellular phones, so I called her on her family home phone, and I sent her gifts, including flowers.

After my relentless pursuit, this young lady gave in and agreed to go on dates with me. Notably, she invited me to her home. Her family showed me much love and were extremely cordial. Their friendliness and caring attitudes toward each other were infectious. There were times when we would sit and talk for hours, sharing birthday celebrations and remembrances. This was the kind of family experience I had been dreaming of. I soon came to realize that much of what they shared was because they were Christians or very religiously persuaded. My admiration for the family grew, especially for Zelpher, who by then I was fully convinced I wanted to be my wife. The more impressed I became with the family, the more my desire grew to be a part of it. I had to face the challenge of the family being regular church attendees, and I was by no means a church-attending person. I questioned whether I would I fit in or whether this would be the end of my chance of having Zelpher as my wife.

At this time, Zelpher's father was still in Jamaica, so I built as close a relationship with her mother as I possibly could. When her dad came from Jamaica, he did not like the idea of me marrying his daughter at all. He thought I was too old for her. I also was already the father of two children with separate mothers. He also could see nothing that I had to offer his daughter, who at the time was still going to high school and had a promising future. I had only a grade-eleven education and was already a struggling father of two, with no major trade or skill. The fact was that I had nothing to lose, while Zelpher could have marred her future. Despite her father's objections, Zelpher and I continued dating each other.

In spite of the very real challenges, this young lady, now my wife, gave me the one-million-dollar surprise when I asked her to marry me and she said yes.

Sometime during this period of dating and courtship, I was invited to attend a church service with a cousin of mine. I said to myself I had nothing to lose, so I went. This began the dramatic change that life offered me. God then became more than just another passing mention to me. I began seeing why my wife's family was such a happy one. A true relationship with God makes the difference.

After I gave my life to the Lord and got baptized, I

became closely associated with the pastor of the church. He had told me even before I became a Christian that God had a calling on my life. I did not pay much attention to that. I laughed and thought it to be just another crazy religious statement. I was baptized in 1996. I immersed myself into church-related activities even though life was still challenging for me economically. To make ends meet, I shared space with one of my cousins; my son and I occupied one bedroom. My daughter visited me periodically. My cousin occupied the other bedroom and had my daughter sleep with her when she visited. In February 1997, I proposed to Zelpher. I made the necessary living arrangements in preparation for the marriage. My young wife would instantaneously become a wife and a mother, even though she did not have a child of her own. This was another act of unpreparedness. My perspectives were now changed; I had now become a practicing, eagerly learning Christian. I no longer wanted to marry my wife just because she was beautiful; I wanted a wife to be everything to me and with me. Nevertheless, I lacked most of the know-how of a counseled, cultured marriage.

To me, her agreement to marry me meant that I had everything I needed to make me happy, but realistically, I was still very unprepared to be her husband. She knew I had not grown to be six feet tall; nor had I developed a singing ability, embarked on a career, or become more handsome. By this time, she was content with all the things I lacked physically; the issue was now my social unpreparedness. During the period of premarital counseling with my pastor, we began to discover that being tall or short and handsome; being able to sing or not; and having beautiful bold eyes, a light complexion, and a nice smell were not the real prerequisites for a successful marriage.

During the period of our premarital counseling, there

were times when we both were unsure of our preparedness for the task of living together as a married couple, let alone being qualified parents. The one thing I did not lose was my passionate love for Zelpher. I was still in love with her. My pastor, our marriage counselor, did not think my wife was ready to take on a husband with two children or the responsibilities of being committed to the principles of being accountable to her husband. He even suggested that we postpone the wedding, which we didn't. Despite all my pastor's concerns, we concluded months of counseling with the decision to get married, and so we did. We had only one sad experience: my wife's father did not attend the wedding.

CHAPTER 2

What Is Marriage? How Did It Come About?

Think Again before You Say "I Do" is written by a Christian minister, a pastor, and counselor of several years. Though not written just for Christians, the book is written from a Christian perspective, with the Bible as its primary reference; therefore, it is based in Christian orthodoxy. Throughout the book, readers will find answers to the question, What is marriage and how did it come about? This question has a foundational answer given in the Bible, in the book of Genesis 2:21–25.

Marriage is not just a law of man; it is the plan of God. Therefore, we should not enter into it unadvisedly or carelessly; rather, we should do so thoughtfully. The couple

Adam and Eve, referenced in the passage that appears in the paragraph above, are, according to the creation story, the first couple to occupy our known world. The major difference between us and the couple in this Genesis account is that neither of these two individuals had to go searching for a mate, while we and many generations before us have been tasked to make our own choices. (I guess those who still practice arranged marriages do have a leg up on the rest of us). It was God who first said it was not good for the man to be alone; so He first went about choosing a partner for the man. He did not choose a partner from any other creature which he had made. Importantly, Scripture says God took a part of man from him to make for him a compatible partner for his well-being. We can see through this act why the right male being matched with the right female is vitally important. For us, compatibility is not discovered just because we choose a mate of our own species, of our own race, of our own ethnicity, or even of our own skin color. We have to discover compatibility through communication. While we do have the right to our personal choices of complexion, height, race, culture, and such, it is generally proven that all these are just face values. To find compatibility, one must be in tune with one's own sense of values and chosen practices. The motivation behind choosing a life mate, or partner, cannot be just about sex, wealth, or even equal educational status. While these all have significant values, they often are secondary to the primal reason for marriage. The full satisfaction of marriage will be enjoyed only when we embrace its original intent.

Marriage Is about the Bigger Picture

Because my wife and I did not discuss issues such as parenting, the sharing of our time, personal likes and dislikes, and social tolerances, we were unprepared to deal maturely with these issues when they did surface.

We had a very turbulent first few years of marriage. The wheels had just about fallen off. You see, when we talk about love, so often we are for the most part centering our feelings on the emotions we feel toward another person sensually. But there is a more lasting pleasure that comes from the inner qualities of your mate. When one discovers qualities in one's partner that incentivize one to work toward greater achievements, a deeper expression of love will most likely result. We all want to feel inspired by the persons we share life's partnership with. The feeling of real connectedness (love) will not be found in the pride of being the man with such a beautiful woman, or the woman with such a wealthy, athletic, tall, handsome, muscular, and charming-looking man. These things have a way of diminishing with time. I myself, when I first saw my wife, felt love at first sight. I can recall the emotions that drove my passion to have her as my wife. As I mentioned before, she was physically attractive, and all my central feelings jumped into motion. When these are the emotions that drive our passions toward a relationship, we more than likely will bypass the more substantial calculations we need to make.

The Bible: A Resource Manual

Whether you are a Christian or not, the Bible is a reliable source of information on relationships; however, there is a pitfall. There are people who carry the Bible but do not know what's in there, and there are those who read the Bible but do not practice what's in it. A person who practices what the Bible teaches about marriage will make a good premarital counselor; seek one out.

There are some myths about marriage. One is that if you are a regular attendee at a church, you are guaranteed to have a happy marriage. Statistics have not borne this out. Church attendants, according to a census, have only about a 10 percent better marriage success rate than those who do not attend church. It is not whether or not one goes to a church that determines whether a marriage will last; it is how two individuals pay attention to the things which promote a healthy relationship. And one of the things that promote a healthy marriage relationship is the practice of a well-thought-out Bible-based marriage plan. This is the discovery I made; my wife and I were ardently going to church, and I had become very active in various Christian lifestyle practices, but my wife and I began disagreeing about everything. Everything had become a problem. My wife was very displeased with the way I managed my time. She was adamant that I was not attentive to her needs. The same man who once was so attached to this light-skinned, bold-eyed beauty was now being accused of being insensitive to her needs. I felt as though the ghost of my father's insensitivity was hounding me. I felt that I was living my childhood all over again. I could hear my mother's voice in my wife's complaints, so

I thought to myself, "What have I done?" The very things that I hated about living with my parents were the things I was now reliving. I became my dad, doing to my wife some of the things he did to my mother. It was at this point I thought I should turn to other married couples in the church for advice. My search led me to discover that there seemed to be not one couple in the church that had the kind of marriage I was looking for. Every couple that I turned to were having challenges of their own. Imagine the surprise I got when I found out that even my pastor's marriage was not perfect.

Now I was perplexed. I asked myself, "If my pastor's marriage is not perfect, and if most of the marriages of those people I admire seem so much in shambles, where do I find help?" I made the decision that I would just adapt to the way of life as everyone else seemed to have been doing. We had a strange relationship of arguing at home and loving at church. This lasted only for so long until I realized that marriages do not fix people, but rather people fix marriages.

One of the ways that I thought of solving the challenges in my marriage then was to tell my wife that I did not want to have children with her because I already had two children with two different mothers. I foresaw a divorce coming and did not want to add children into the mix.

The Next Step

In spite of my confused life with my wife, my faith in God was growing deeper. I was very passionate about a life of prayer and a good relationship with God. I soon became tired of seeing love and hatred trying to coexist. By reading the Bible, I began to believe that God could help my wife and me if we really wanted our marriage to work out.

Zelpher and I decided to go for marriage counseling. It was not about whether or not we were to get married;

it was about what we needed to do to stay married. My wife was not keen on sharing our personal differences with anyone, so even though we went for counseling, she was hesitant to speak to the counselor about the things we were arguing about. I, on the other hand, talked about everything. My wife became even more distant in the relationship. Cuddling was no longer a part of our nighttime experiences. She was on one side of the bed, at a distance, and I on the other. Touching her was a forbidden act. Now I had to face the hard question of what I was to do.

"Think again before you say 'I do'" was not yet a part of my vocabulary!

I had by this time developed friendships with other wonderful young ladies within the church. My mind began drifting with thoughts, and I was questioning myself as to whether I had made the right decision in marrying my wife. I did not want to get a divorce, but with all the unsettled feelings and unpredictable actions coming from my wife, emotionally I was in turmoil. Through all of this, the one thing I had hope in was that God could help us, so I clung to my relationship with God. Unknown to me then was that God had a planned way out for my wife and me. God certainly brought us through, and today, after those storms and many other challenges, we are still together, in love.

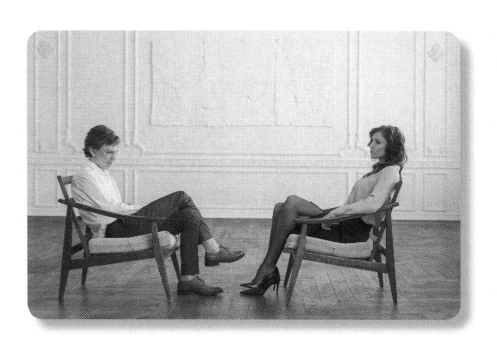

CHAPTER 3

The Importance of Shared Values

Transparency

In Amos 3:3, the question is asked, "how may two walk together, if they are not in agreement?" In Proverbs 13:12, the wise King Solomon states that "Hope deferred maketh the heart sick; but when the desire cometh, it is a tree of life"(KJV). I will be bold and say that every couple enters into marriage with expectations. Our expectations usually channel us into hoping for a preferred outcome. Sadly, many married couples enter into marriage expecting things solely on the basis of assumptions. This is like sitting in a car and expecting that because it is a car with an engine, it will get you where you want to go without a driver. Couples often assume that because the other person behaves so nicely in one situation, that person will be same in all other situations. For one to expect a particular outcome, one needs to apply the formula necessary to produce that outcome. For one partner to be expected to meet the needs of the other, clear requests need to be made by the person who has the expectation. Likes and dislikes are often based on personal values, and because individual values are very important and may vary from person to person, transparency is necessary. This understanding should be a cardinal one when one contemplates a proposal for marriage.

Let's consider that as distinctly as we are defined by our fingerprints, we can be equally different regarding the things that matter to us. We should never assume that a person is going to automatically think the way we would want him or her to. Therefore, it is necessary for couples to have in-depth discussions on the values that are mutually important to them.

Couples should always remember that habits and personal traits do not change just because two become married, and greater conflict may arise if you begin to express expectations after you are married. This will be so especially in situations where there was no stated position during premarital discussions. *Think Again before You Say "I Do"* is written primarily to correct some of these mistakes before they happen.

Because marriage is supposed to be a commitment between a man and a woman for a lifetime partnership, it is not to be entered into without the searching out of individual long-term goals, values, and aspirations. There is necessary advice which should be sought before you say "I do," so couples should seek the council of a trained qualified marriage counselor. A duly trained counselor will ask you to state your goals and values, and will steer a couple toward supporting each other's goals. I strongly advise couples to seek out counselors who share their basic values and are also capable of suggesting new ways of achieving mutual goals.

Because our decisions can be influenced by the different experiences we've had, it is important for couples who are contemplating marriage to discuss past experiences. It is not uncommon to find individuals whose approaches to marriage have been shaped by experiences they either have had personally or have witnessed.

As a pastor, I have been privileged to counsel many married couples who, after many years of marriage, have not been able to let go of the negative opinions they have formed about the opposite sex. Such couples' approaches to marriage have been shaped by fear. Because they have witnessed infidelity in the marriage of a friend or even a family member, their fear is that this will also happen to them. Oftentimes this fear can also be planted by someone's negative counsel. A friend whose former or present spouse cheated in their marriage is prone to give negative counsel to one who is planning to be married. A parent who went through a divorce will more than likely counsel a son or daughter to not be trusting in a relationship. Great care must be taken when couples are seeking advice concerning marriage. Because trust is an essential value to a marriage, this should be discussed as thoroughly as possible. Couples should not be afraid to explore with each other to the extent to which they themselves may have compromised the health of a past relationship. This does not mean that one should never engage in a relationship with one who has been unfaithful in a previous relationship, but there should be transparency. Many individuals have developed more honest behaviors because of losses suffered due to past mistakes or infidelity. Many such individuals have sought and received counsel that has helped them become more honest and conscientious partners. Not only should one expect transparency; one should also be transparent. If one is harboring negative feelings in regard to trusting, one owes it to the other person to be transparent about that fear.

Finances

It is generally acknowledged that money is one of the most common reasons for the breakups of marriages. So often during the period of courtship, one partner will say to the other, "It does not matter how much you are earning; we will make it work." A term that is often used is "I'm not fussy." Then the couple marry and find that the demands dictate a different response. Couples must always look ahead and plan realistically. Wisdom and money make a good defense. Spoken love does not fulfill financial responsibilities. Couples should not allow nostalgic feelings and the desire to be with each other to infringe upon the necessity of financial discussions before marriage.

How couples treat the matter of finance management is crucial to the future health of their marriage. Both in courtship and during marriage counseling, the parties should investigate each other's financial management habits and come to an agreed-upon protocol for future financial responsibility. Future assessment should also be made if there needs to be a change in the agreement. Old habits should be given priority only if they are deemed satisfactory by both parties. As individuals, we live our lives the way we see fit. When we become married, we affect each other through whatever habits we have already formed. Remember: we are talking about marriage. This means merging lives. Couples cannot just choose to be what each wants to be; if that is to be the case, then singleness for such persons is to be preferable.

If you have been a compulsive spender all your life,

you should not be the manager of the family finances. If you have the tendency to want your way with everything, you should not be the finance manager of the family. It is very important to engage a financial planner to give advice at the onset of a marriage. Bear in mind that just as in the case of fidelity, honesty about debts is extremely important when discussing the plan for marriage. The treatment of money has been one of the greater causes of divorce. Partners are prone to hide their financial debts in order to preserve their relationships. This, however, is just as dishonest as overstating financial holdings. Always remember that the rights to a marriage are not gained by dishonesty and pretension; they are gained by true love, honesty, and transparency.

Intimacy

Marriages will succeed or fail based on the level of intimacy couples enjoy. The issue of failure comes primarily because partners fail to discuss their expectations during courtship. Charles Dickens left us this quote: "… in a word, I was too cowardly to do what I knew to be right, and I had been too cowardly to avoid doing what I knew to be wrong." To expect something from another without stating your preferences is, in many ways, selfish. To avoid the heartache of unmet expectations, couples should not avoid making their desires known for any reason. Your partner might not be able, or may choose not to, acquiesce to your requests or demands, but you will not know his or her response until you have either made the request or stated your expectation or preference. The subject of sexual preferences is of major importance; therefore, couples should not shy away from this discussion. Your marriage counselor should give this discussion equal priority to discussions on money and other primary matters.

Sometimes partners are reluctant to initiate the conversation on this subject, but this is too major a subject to not have clear understanding on it before marriage. Not all couples engage in sexual encounters before marriage. And even for those who do so, sometimes the encounters are infrequent enough for the partners to disguise their preferences. Adjustments are oftentimes made after couples are married and are comfortable with each other. Exploring different experiences often happen after couples have been able to talk through the reasons for their fears, resistance, or reticence. Because the pleasure of intimacy should be a shared experience, couples should spare no disclosure of their likes or dislikes before getting into marriage. In the case where one partner may be entering upon his or her first sexual encounter, gentle coaching may be necessary, and this should be undertaken by the experienced partner. Remember that for many individuals, the first experience can either make or break the romance.

Since intimacy is not all about the physical act of the sexual encounter and males and females most times have different desires relating to lovemaking and foreplay, the subject should be discussed as thoroughly as possible. Do not forget that it's not all about you. The beauty of marriage lies in the proper understanding of partnership and mutual benefits. Couples must therefore gain an understanding of each other's desires, preferences, nuances, and priorities. The understanding or knowledge gained in these discussions will become useful in the cultivating of a culture for your marital pleasures and enjoyment. Life is much more pleasant when partners are thinking in sync with each other.

Interactions within the Family Structure.

The pleasure of a lasting family relationship is dependent upon which decisions are made by couples. This is a subject that requires serious consideration. Considering the broader scope of people who are or can be considered a part of the family structure, and understanding that not all individuals can be trusted to observe boundaries, couples need to lay out an agreed-upon set of rules by which the family will be guided. Firstly, the married couple must decide the kind of relationship they will share as it relates to decision-making in the household and with the family at large. As was mentioned before, partnership goes a long way toward the maintaining of a "happy home" marriage.

There are several things to take into consideration regarding the above: shared responsibilities, parenting, dealing with the blended family, determining who goes to work outside the home, dealing with the in-laws, determining how decisions are made, and establishing where to go for advice. I will deal with each of these items separately.

Shared Responsibilities.

Couples should anticipate potential situations that may arise in a marriage and discuss possible solutions. There are expected and unexpected occurrences that come with relationships. Each individual has likes and dislikes, and our willingness to do certain things or chores can be based on any number of factors, including whether or not we like doing a particular thing. The way in which duties are divided cannot always be determined by one being male or female; therefore, practical approaches should be applied. Discussion is a means by which solutions are discovered; therefore, couples should talk about things that potentially or necessarily will occur. Adjustments can always be made, and partners should be prepared for them. Remember that love shares. All unions create added responsibilities; therefore, the couple in the union should shoulder these responsibilities.

Based on the way individuals were brought up regarding culture, economic status, or some other dynamic, their approaches to role sharing may differ. Mutual understanding should be employed to address the demands created by the present reality. If you were brought up in a privileged lifestyle, where everything was provided or done for you, that doesn't mean that your partner must be expected to provide you with the same coverage. Marriage means entering a new reality in which your mate is not your paid household helper. You are now one of the providers as well as one of the helpers in the family.

Where cultural differences are involved; it is advisable that if you desire to maintain the practices of your culture, you should consider marrying within that culture, where the knowledge of these expectations is already grounded. It is never reasonable to seek to enter into a mutual relationship with a cultural bias. Remember: marriage is a union of two equal partners, not a dictator and a subject. Roles can be determined by schedules, finances, or any dynamic which may dictate the particular arrangements, but the greatest determining factor should be love and mutual agreement.

Parenting

Parents should never assume that they have all the know-how of parenting. A good idea would be that couples attend a parenting class before the birth of a child, especially in cases where neither partner has parented before. And even in cases where one or both parents have had children, it should not be assumed that parenting styles are alike. It is then necessary for couples to discuss their values regarding parenting. Planning one's family has not been done well until parenting values have been discussed and developed. Couples should bear in mind always that we, for the most part, are shaped by our experiences. Each partner may want to parent the way he or she was parented. This could be a major conflict. Here is where compromise might be most needed. Discussing mutual values is a good place to start, but never disregard the learn-as-you-go factor.

Blended Family

We are living in a time when a blended family lifestyle is more of a possibility than not. This sometimes requires more negotiations. The discipline under which the family will operate should always be discussed in blended-family situations. The values by which the already parenting partner and child had been living must now be understood by the nonparenting partner. The child's needs should be at the center of all discussions. The child, however, cannot be the one making the decisions regarding the value system the family will operate on. In the case of a blended family, both parents should be very careful not to insist on maintaining things just the way they were. Attention should be given to the concerns of the other partner, should they exist. In the case of adult children who do not have special needs, they should be encouraged to move on their own immediately. And in cases where immediate transition is not possible, steps should be taken to ensure that this be done at the earliest possible time. Couples should discuss this transition and work with the child to ensure new living arrangements are made. Bear in mind that being in love does not cancel all the anxieties that come with newlyweds integrating their lives, so all additional stresses should be minimized. Too many couples have not survived the stresses resulting from the extra baggage that came along in such situations. This is also the case with the stresses relating to in-laws.

In-Laws

The place of in-laws in a family has been in discussion for generations. The role in-laws play can be either helpful or very destructive. Some in-laws seem to consider it their dedication to interfere in the daily lives of newlywed couples. There is hardly anything more necessary in the life of a newly married couple than that of setting boundaries against in-law dominance. It is very common for an in-law to think she or he knows best; mothers-in-law oftentimes try to instruct a wife as to how she must treat her husband. The fear is that she wants to impose her concept of what caring for her son was, not giving thought to the reality that he is now living not with his mother but with his wife. Mothers-in-law who have been the dominant figures in a marriage will want to see those same powers manifested in their daughter's marriage. Some fathers-in-law will want to impose the same attitudes upon a son or daughter- in- law. Couples must take care to understand that a marriage is between two—one and one's mate—not between one and one's parents or other siblings. A married couple's in-laws should be treated with respect, but not to the disrespect or dishonor of one's partner. The boundaries should be agreed upon by both partners and should not be violated to make a parent or sibling happy. Always remember to whom you are married.

Take particular care about your living arrangements. It is, for the most part, unadvisable to share a dwelling with in-laws, especially in-law parents. If you have to share living arrangements with your in-laws, it should be for the shortest period possible.

How Decisions Are Made and Who Makes Them

When couples are contemplating a marriage covenant, they should consider erasing any previous habit of manipulation. Just as the decision to get married is a joint affair, except in cases where arranged marriages are acceptable, couples must embrace the principle of partnership. It does not matter whether one partner is wealthier, more educated, older, or whatever the notable distinction may be. Marriage is a partnership. the institution of marriage is not like a company in which there is a senior partner and a junior partner, or a managing partner and a limited partner, allowing for one to be above the other in power and responsibilities. This is why couples make pledges to each other during the marriage ceremony. They each agree to take the other on as a life partner. Both commit to support each other exclusively. In the culture of marriage in which this author exists, it is primarily accepted among the broader population that marriage is a joint partnership. If we consider that love is not selfish, not manipulative, and not arrogant, then a good distinction for love is that it shares.

Decisions at any level are more easily embraced when

individuals are considered integral in their making. In marriage, therefore, decisions should be made on the basis of equal partnership. Even in cases in which one partner's suggestion might not carry weight in the decision, when respect is shown for another's opinion, cooperation is more easily embraced.

When seeking advice, financial or otherwise, it is recommended that couples seek out professional counselors. If this is not possible because of economic reasons, then go to someone neutral. Avoid giving the opportunity for partiality. If you are a Christian, seek out someone within the fellowship of your church. Your pastor may be connected with good counselors even outside the church community. Never be too proud to seek sound counseling or advice. Make a mutual commitment to not enter into financial dealings with in-laws if at all possible, as this could expose you to manipulation. I'll talk more about this later.

CHAPTER 4

It has been said that "a good relationship starts with good communication." When couples respect each other enough, everything is important for sharing. For every relationship to have true success, there needs to be mutual respect. This begins with not assuming that what you think is important is the opinion of your spouse or partner. Couples must give each other the right to say yes, or no, when the decision in the making will impact both parties. Good communication can result in positive reactions even when the news is not positive. As couples learn to share their thoughts, expectations, and fears, partners can respond to more than what is presented outwardly. Good communication oftentimes reveals the inner feelings of the one who speaks. Considering that partnership means helping each other to make hard things less burdensome, couples should consider how and what they communicate with each other. Timing is also a factor as to how information is sought, shared, and digested. Urgent matters should be treated with urgency, but couples should have some agreement on how and when things are considered urgent. The obvious scenarios will generally speak for themselves.

Couples often enter into marriage with questions about each other and neglect to ask those questions because of fear that they may offend the other person even though the matter is important in deciding on a long-term marriage relationship. During courtship or dating is the appropriate time to ask your questions. If the matter is of significant concern to you, you should never be afraid to ask about it. Remember: it is better not to enter into a permanent relationship with unanswered questions—especially the ones that were never asked. This will prevent you from trying to fit yourself into a mold in which you will never find comfort.

Pondering the Hard Questions

The questions surrounding one's health may seem an imposition, but they must be asked. There are many health issues that may come into play when you engage in marriage: sexually transmitted diseases are common, and although most of these diseases are curable and should not be viewed as a reason why couples should abandon the plan for marriage, each individual should be aware whether the other has ever contracted an STD. There should be absolute openness about the subject. Remember: this is an issue that can affect whether or not bearing or producing children is possible.

Couples should discuss hereditary family traits. If one partner does not volunteer such information, then the other should by all means ask about it. Some individuals do not like to revisit their past, but the only questions that should not be matters of discussion are those that definitely will not affect the other person. Partners who have had several sex partners should be willing to share with their new potential partners the history of their past, especially if they had same-gender relationships. Not everyone may be as liberal as you are, or as you may have been. Each partner should be willing to disclose any such relationships and then allow the other to make a fair decision while not being judgmental. Remember: your questions are to inform your decision, not to encourage you to judge the other person's character.

Preferences in Sexual Practices

Honest discussions should be had as to one's method and frequency relating to sexual activities. One partner should not assume how often the other will want to be involved sexually. Your need may be different from your partner's. Before you enter into marriage, this is a practical discussion to have. Remember: not every two persons are alike.

There are some outcomes of sexual practices that are going to be totally dependent upon your agreed-upon preferences. For Christian couples, your religious beliefs may well inform your practices of choice. As a pastor, I have always encouraged couples to explore acceptable practices that will keep their marriage pleasures enjoyable. There are also a number of books by experts that may inform your decisions for pleasureful intimacy and health.

A Marriage Nightmare

Avoid every inclination to compare your mate with a past mate. Do not be too quick to tell your partner how much he or she reminds you of your former partner or spouse. Even when it is true, treat your mate as an individual, keep the comparisons out. If you are pursuing a relationship which you would like to result in marriage, ex-mate is still a part of your thoughts, you should put this new relationship on hold until you have dealt with the reasons for your thoughts. Do not try to use one individual to cancel the other from your mind. Unresolved issues are not that easily overcome. A good question to ask your new mate is, "What would you like to know about me and my past. When you have included your past as being open for questions, the new person in the relationship will be more likely to ask the questions that are important. This may also make it easier for you to ask questions which you would like to have answers to. Remember that, expectations, and poor communication can be the undoing of a relationship, so ask your questions, while at the same time being respectful of your partner's feelings.

Avoid Manipulation

If you have found that your partner is vulnerable in any area in the relationship, do not use that vulnerability as a bargaining chip. Do not use the threat of breaking off the relationship to get your mate to say what you want to hear. To do this may come back to hurt you later. Let the relationship survive on total honesty. If in the beginning you discover that you are more financially stable than your partner, do not use your financial power as a negotiating tool. Relationships should be built on love and respect. This is not possible where honesty is absent. This is not only so now, but later in your marriage you may be inclined to make this a practice.

Some folks take a bit more time than others to open up, so patience should be extended so each partner can lose his or her fears. Oftentimes individuals are afraid they'll say the wrong things, so if you detect hesitancy in your partner to address the questions you may want to have answers to, use whatever honest means you have to alleviate those fears. You may be doing yourself a favor.

When What You Fear Becomes Your Mistake

When one feels so in love that he or she avoids being truthful about the past or in answering a question about the future, this oftentimes become known. At such a time, trust can be detrimentally eroded. It is said in some quarters, "Do now and ask for forgiveness later." This might be an idea for some situations, but not for marriage. Even people who are not themselves honest look for honesty in others and also find it hard to forgive dishonesty. When dishonesty is discovered in the later stages of a relationship, it may not result in a marriage breakup, but it may cause irreparable damage to your partner's trust in you. As a counselor, I've always said, "It is better to lose a relationship early by telling the truth than to build a house upon a false statement and lose your investments later."

Avoid the Temptation to Be Secretive

Many people believe and promote the idea of "don't ask, don't tell." I do not recommend this principle as a recipe for a happy home. We sometimes subscribe to the idea that what's in the past should stay in the past. While we do not live in the past, the effects of past experiences do oftentimes travel with us. The partners we couple our lives with should be ones we can be open with. If we have to keep secrets about us sacred, then we should avoid committing to that relationship. Remember: the person you intend to get into marriage with should be one you can share your joys and disappointments with. Your partner should be your confidant. Practice the talk and listen rule.

CHAPTER 5

Respecting Rights and Feelings

Considering the emotional "feelings" of your partner is as important as protecting your own feelings. One of the main drivers of hurt feelings is the relationship with ex-partners. Because children are often a part of past relationships, the accountable partner needs to give great consideration to the kind of relationship that is maintained with the former partner. Some relationships might not have ended acrimoniously, so there might well be lingering unresolved feelings in one or both parties. This should not be carried into a new relationship. If you are unsure of how you feel intimately about the person you were once with, those feelings should be resolved before entering a new relationship. Sometimes we may think we are through with a certain relationship, and we may even have verbal agreement with a former partner that the relationship is over, but then come those lingering emotional feelings each time there is an encounter with that person.

So, to prevent past emotions affecting a new relationship, each individual needs to clearly understand that the past is the past. Every effort must be made to clarify with the former partner, and with your new partner, where you stand. Acknowledging to your new partner that there are unresolved feelings existing in you for the person you were with before may pave the way for a true resolution. If the matter is discussed and an understanding is arrived at, each party should respect the feelings of the other and not breach those conclusions. One should not facilitate encounters with a former spouse or partner that will cause conflicts in the new relationship. The plans for how to deal with stepchildren, especially those who are on a court-appointed or mutual-agreement visitation regimen should be a priority. Former spouses and former partners often use the guise of "children needing their two parents" to lure ex-partners back into intimate encounters.

Agreement about contacts with a former partner should be fully discussed, and proper boundaries should be established and kept.

Some Important Rules to Observe

1. Don't plan one-on-one social meetings with former spouses or partners without the agreement of your new partner.

2. As much as is possible, avoid private dinners, lunches, or other engagements with your former partner.

3. Don't discuss your partner's weaknesses with a former partner or spouse.

4. Don't entertain questions comparing your present and former partner or spouse.

5. Do not invite your former partner or spouse to dinner, especially if you are aware of any lingering feelings of intimacy.

6. Keep your spouse's or partner's feelings in mind at all times; don't think your partner is just too sensitive.

7. Don't engage in sexual talk or reminiscence of past enjoyments or experiences with a former spouse or partner. Don't wish that things were the same with your present spouse. Discover new experiences with your new mate and enjoy them; create new memories with the one you are with.

8. Even if you would not disapprove of your partner maintaining a close relationship with a former partner or spouse, remember that your partner is not you.

Give Each Other a Listening Ear

As it is with good communication, respecting each other enough to listen to a complaint, the expression of one's feeling, or the sharing of a thought, makes for a good or better relationship. One great passage of the Bible says, "One should be swift to listen, and slow to speak" (James 1:19).

A quote from Bryant H. McGill states, "One of the most sincere forms of respect is actually listening to what another has to say." In every great relationship, one of the most beautiful things is to know you have a mate who listens. It is not always that one is looking to another for a solution, but one is looking for two ears and one heart to listen. Listening gives you an opportunity to make a difference in your mate's life. It could be a matter totally unrelated to you that your mate wants to share; it could also be about you, the children, an in-law, or anything about that day. Make time for listening. Don't be quick to dismiss a conversation. Don't be quick to give an answer to a question you didn't hear fully.

Avoid being unsympathetic to your mate because you don't see the point of his or her concerns. Never disregard your mate's input in the plans for your family; everyone has a right to be heard. When someone seems emotional about a matter that you are undisturbed about, seek to ascertain the reason for those emotions. Sometimes past experiences are brought back by present realities. You may be the one to make some sense of the matter and help your partner to recover and rejuvenate.

If you are asked to revisit an old matter, exercise some patience, and if you are not able to at the moment, then offer to listen at another time, and be faithful to your promise. The way you respond may be the difference maker. When there is a need to correct an action, put yourself in the position of the other person, and speak in the way you would appreciate being spoken to. I have shared this counsel with many: "When a matter becomes an offence, do not focus on who is wrong, focus on what the matter is." This gives a chance for both parties to agree on the solution. We should endeavor not to speak attackingly to our mates. If you have an occasion to be upset about a matter or an action, first consider how your speech will affect your mate or what will result from the way you confront him or her. At the same time, always remember that to confront a matter or an action done by your mate is the best means of arriving at an objective end. When respect is shown in the way we confront, our mates will be more likely to submit, if submission is needed. Never speak to your make as though you are addressing a child. No one likes to feel demeaned.

Practice the principle of complimenting before pointing out faults. Remember that in "the best of us there are some weaknesses, and in the worst of us, there are virtues." Do not let criticism destroy an otherwise good relationship.

Practice complimenting over complaining.

When spouses seek out good for each other, they will be good together. There is a verse of wisdom that says that "two are better than one." For those who are religious, here is a warning! Do not believe that because you are very religious you are immune from disagreements. Remember that we were humans first before we became religious, and now that we are religious, our individual brains have not stopped working. We still have thoughts, preferences, emotions, and even a little pride. As you contemplate the many decisions facing you, such as where you want to live, how many children you want to have, which relationships you want to keep, how to treat in-laws, and, very importantly, which church you want to attend, keep in mind that marriage is a partnership.

It is the institution wherein the scriptures declare that two are made one. This asks for mutual understanding and a mutual respect for each other's contribution to the process. Plan a time for the proper discussion on each of these important aspects of your life. The more united you are in making the decisions, the less likely you are to be drawn into individual regrets. When together you make the decisions, together you can fix the unforeseen challenges. Remember: respect, respect, respect. If love covers a multitude of sins, then respect prevents them from happening.

How We Choose Friends

Most people enter their marriages already having their circle of friends. For those who are religious, their friends can be from the church they attend; others may have friends from work and other groups, religious and nonreligious. Sometimes the two who are to be married are mostly involved with people from the same circle of friends. In the case where two are already familiar with the same people, mutual respect in the relationships may not be hard. However, now that you are entering into a marriage relationship, changes may be necessary. Much consideration must be given to how your time is spent. Neither party should expect that former friends will automatically fall away like leaves in the fall, and neither party should necessarily expect to conduct life the same as before, especially if one partner was more outgoing than the other.

It becomes necessary for the parties, at the onset of marriage planning, to include the friendship discussion in the mix. Due consideration must now be given to how you choose the friends you desire to keep mutually. Remember: your marriage is to be between you and your partner, not you and anyone else. Respect must be given to the right of demand brought on by marriage. Some folks get married and still want to behave single. Keep it straight! "Marriage is for a couple; single is for one." Not all friends are respectful of the necessary changes a marriage demands, so both parties need to be selective as to whom they try to keep as family friends. Friends should help to strengthen you in your marriage, not weaken the bond of your marriage

CHAPTER 6

The Value of Consistency

In every successful marriage, you will find the valuable threads of consistency. Because we are wired to be more content with knowing what to expect, each partner in a marriage relationship should embrace an acceptable moral code. "Consistency can either be positive or negative." This chapter examines codes of ethics and some acceptable social behaviors that are important and necessary for a marriage to succeed.

As I have said before, each person comes to a marriage with already developed habits and personality traits. During our developing years, we pick up habits and cultivate traits that may be consistent with us but are not conducive to a good marriage experience. Even though partners have gone through several months of premarital counseling and have spent time together, some of the habits and traits which are not tolerable for you might not be detected until you are cohabiting. It is true that some partners may disguise these traits and or habits because they have had difficulties with them in past relationships.

If a partner is going to be consistently selfish, not willing to share in household chores while at the same time expecting the other partner to be at his or her best, this will create problems in the marriage. If while you are dating, your partner exhibits any of these behaviors, you should call it what it is and not allow continuation of it into the marriage.

If the behavior is discovered after you are already married, then address it allowing your partner to know that such an attitude or practice is not okay with you. Be watchful of how your mate speaks to you, whether in public or private. Accept only those behaviors in courtship that you are prepared to accept during marriage. Too often people wait until marriage to begin trying to correct intolerable behaviors. If you have already married someone you felt was not behaving in a manner toward you as you would have wished, it will be harder for you to correct this.

Some bad habits may also be developed during the course of your marriage. Some partners and spouses become complacent in their relationships. They may have observed certain behavioral traits in one or both of their parents and adapted that behavior to their relationships. Some may also use the secretive and subtle method of not displaying the quality or trait until they are comfortably in the relationships. Whatever the reason for the detachment from the former norm or the display of an unsuitable norm, you should not accept the behavior if it is unsettling to you. Be willing to discuss how the action impacts you and the changes you are requiring and expecting. Be willing to work with your mate for a better outcome.

Some persons have bad financial habits; their spending habits have gotten them into financial distress before, but they have not adapted to new methods and disciplines. In such a case, you should invite your partner into a meaningful discussion, discuss a change in your family financial management, and, if necessary, invite your partner to pursue good financial planning counseling. It is better to suggest changes than to sit and suffer through, hoping for a change while saying nothing.

Some couples cease some of the social and intimate gestures that may have been common for them during courtship. There are no more good-bye kisses, and no more opening of building doors, car doors, and so forth. They are not bringing flowers home anymore even though the finances are still there. The things they previously discussed are being done independent of each other now. Terms of endearment are dropped, and first names are again used. All these things are inconsistent with what used to be, and there seems not to be any explanation for the changes. Partners need to confront the disappearance of those realities and make a conscious effort to repair those things that are meaningful to the marriage relationship.

There are times when the changes in behaviors are troubling to both parties, and if one partner does not initiate a reconciliation, it is never discovered that both parties have been thinking that the other has changed. One thing is always certain: whenever consistency is changed to inconsistency, it is always noticed.

Spirituality Matters

It is generally known that those who believe in a spiritual or religious lifestyle are not immune to disagreements and even inconsistencies. When married partners fundamentally and mutually subscribe to a spiritual lifestyle, consistency is generally maintained. As a Christian minister of religion and a pastor of a congregation, I can tell you that my spiritual (religious) beliefs have strongly contributed to my desire to be consistent.

Firstly, I learn to give to my wife what I desire her to give to me. This means I am always looking for ways to ensure that she is happy. Please don't misunderstand; we cannot account totally for our partner's happiness, but we, by our actions, can contribute to either its maintenance or its destruction. We need to question what will happen if one partner is consistently disruptive in a marriage. Almost in the same breath, we can conclude what will happen when one marriage partner is consistently encouraging or pleasant. Relationships of any kind thrive on positive consistency.

Secondly, when two partners believe in the power of prayer, it releases a sense of peaceful embrace in the relationship. It is generally acknowledged that even folks who do not practice a strict adherence to religion agree that a belief in a deity (God) more often than not brings peace in the relationship.

In every onset of a digression from the agreed-upon

covenants, the observing partner needs to lovingly call the other into accountability.

The Danger of Social Suffocation

Partners are always to be aware that while they are married, most everyone likes to have a friend who is not one's married partner. While care must be given that one does not replace one's partner with an outside friend, each spouse needs to give space for the other to develop friendships. Friendships are developed through work relationships, through communication with former college mates, and sometimes just by accidentally meeting someone through an unplanned occasion.

Spouses are to develop confidence in their relationship; this may take time in such a way that they do not suffocate their partner socially. Unreasonable jealousy is an expression of lack of trust, but it is more of an insecurity in oneself, more often than not, and should not be allowed to stifle an otherwise good relationship. Remember: selfishness manifests itself in many disguises.

If you are feeling an extra sense of anxiety about a friendship that has developed or is developing between your spouse and someone else, you should always admit it and talk it over with your spouse. Discussing these feelings can many times deepen intimacy between partners. Be a best friend to your partner and maintain the confidence of a secured marriage.

Spouses, however, must be careful not to develop such a relationship with an opposite-sex friend until it becomes bothersome to the other. Your marriage must be kept unchallenged from the potential of an intruding other. God has established marriage expressly for procreation and companionship. The man needs his wife for pleasureful companionship, and the woman needs her husband for support and pleasureful companionship. Both are equal in the sight of God.

It is my prayer that as you read this book, your plans for marriage will find new meaning; if you are already married, my prayer is that the thoughts you now think will motivate you to rejuvenate your marriage. Remember: good communication makes for an enjoyable marriage.

Phrases of Endearment for Couples

"Honey, you are the neck that spins my head."

"Honey, you are the oxygen in my lungs."

"Honey, your tongue is as sweet as honey."

"Honey, every time I look at you, my heart skips a beat."

"Honey, your skin is as smooth as silk and as soft as velvet."

"If loving you is wrong, I don't want to be right."

"Honey, your lips are my moisturizer."

"Honey, I found the missing link to my soul, which is you."

"You are my sunshine on a cloudy day."

"Darling, you are the milk in my coffee."

"Honey, we are like peas in a pod, so when you shake, I shake."

"Honey, you are my Miss Universe."

"Honey, you mesmerize my soul."

"Baby, you have the ability to raise the dead."

"Baby, you are the thermostat in our house."

"Roses are red, violets are blue, sugar is sweet, but not sweet as you."

"Darling, every time I look at you, I know God as drawn you and erased the mistakes."

"Baby, you are the butter on my bread."

"Baby, you are the best thing to happen to me since sliced bread."

"Baby, you have discovered the path to my heart."

NOTES

NOTES

NOTES

NOTES

NOTES

Printed in the United States
by Baker & Taylor Publisher Services